Copyright © 2018 Patrick A. Hegarty.

All rights reserved. No part of this publication may be reproduced, distributed or transmitted in any form or by any means, including photocopying, recording, or other electronic or mechanical methods, without the prior written permission of Patrick Hegarty, except in the case of brief quotations embodied in critical reviews and certain other noncommercial uses permitted by copyright law. For permission requests, email the author, with subject line "Attention: Permissions Enquiry" at the email address below.

admin@spiritandtruth.net.au

www.spiritandtruth.net.au

Scriptures quoted from: New International Version of the Bible. Scripture taken from the Holy Bible, NEW INTERNATIONAL VERSION®. Copyright ©1973, 1978, 1984 International Bible Society. All rights reserved throughout the world. Used by permission of International Bible Society.

Scripture quotations identified MSG are from The Message. Copyright © 1993, 1994, 1995 by Eugene Peterson. Used by permission of NavPress Publishing Group.

Any internet addresses (websites, blogs, etc.) in this book are offered as a resource. They are not intended in any way to be or imply an endorsement by Patrick Hegarty, nor does Patrick Hegarty vouch for the content of these sites for the life of this book.

Contents

Using the Daily Journal & Workbook v

Group Session – (INTRODUCTIONS) 1

Group Session – (DEPTH OF CALLING) 7

   [1.1] Depth of calling 8

   [1.2] The need to re:FOCUS 10

   [1.3] Impressive or impacting 12

   [1.4] Life in God's garden 14

   [1.5] Walking and working in the garden 16

   [1.6] The relational rhythm 18

Group Session – (re:FOCUS ON CHRIST) 19

   [2.1] First 20

   [2.2] Getting derailed 22

   [2.3] Abiding 24

   [2.4] Changing lenses 26

   [2.5] re:FOCUS on Christ 28

   [2.6] Living from Christ 30

Group Session – (re:FOCUS ON CHARACTER) 33

   [3.1] I have made you 36

   [3.2] Stuck in a moment 38

   [3.3] Growing character 40

   [3.4] The fruit of perseverance 42

   [3.5] The wilderness effect 44

   [3.6] re:FOCUS on character 46

Group Session – (re:FOCUS ON PEOPLE) **47**

[4.1] People are your purpose 48

[4.2] Your area of influence 50

[4.3] You and the church... 52

[4.4] Oikos – who you do life with 54

[4.5] Your tribe... 56

[4.6] re:FOCUS on people.. 58

Group Session – (re:FOCUS ON TALENT) **59**

[5.1] re:FOCUS on talent 60

[5.2] Put your soul into it 62

[5.3] The heart speaks 64

[5.4] The need at hand 66

[5.5] Spiritual gifts 68

[5.6] When doing for God isn't enough 70

Group Session – (re:FOCUS ON CALLING) **72**

A Plan to re:FOCUS **75**

Re:FOCUS on God - Purpose 1 & 2 75

Re:FOCUS on Character - Purpose 3 & 4.. 77

Re:FOCUS on People - Purpose 5 & 6... 79

Re:FOCUS on Calling - Purpose 7 & 8 82

Other important areas in which to re:FOCUS 83

Notes from your Retreat.. **85**

Using the Daily Journal & Workbook

This Daily Journal & Workbook is a companion of the book *re:FOCUS*.

At the end of each chapter of *re:FOCUS* a response question is asked which assists you in the personal application of the principles mentioned.

This workbook provides an easy way to log your responses in order and have quick access to them during small group meetings.

For Use as a Daily Journal

Each chapter of the book has a dedicated section in this workbook. Simply look up the appropriate chapter number in the Contents section and write down your thoughts and responses.

For Use as a Small Group Workbook

If you are working through this material as a group, there are Group Session notes included to guide your discussion. The Daily Journal pages are sandwiched within these group sessions to ensure easy reference to your responses during group meetings.

INTRODUCTIONS

Group Session

Spend some time going around the group, hearing the names, family details and life context of each participant.

Q. What would you like to get from this course?

_____

_____

ABOUT RE:FOCUS

READ TOGETHER:

Welcome to re:FOCUS. This course is to equip you in taking up your calling in Christ.

Dwell on that statement for a moment. As a believer, your calling is only found in Christ. To be *in* Christ your calling must come *from* Him, be fueled *by* Him, and be fulfilled *for* Him. In short, your calling is not just about you!

For us to discover and walk in God's plan for us we must see beyond ourselves and refocus on the things that matter in God's overall vision. It is when we choose to alter our focus in this way, that new possibilities open up.

How to go through material:

There are six daily readings per week to process and respond to. Do one per day only, as you will need to meditate on and process the concepts slowly. Fill in the Your response section slowly, reflectively and honestly, or you won't receive the full benefit of the process.

In your group meetings your facilitator will help you process and apply the week's concepts.

Group agreement

For your group to be safe and effective, you will need to agree on how you will interact and honour each other. Talk through together which boundaries you may want to have in place for the duration of the course. Below are some suggestions and you can add your own.

Group attendance

We will honour each other by being on time and regularly attending meetings.

Safe environment

We will create a place where each person is protected and loved, free to share without judgment or unsolicited advice.

Respect differences

We will be gentle and gracious to those with different spiritual maturity, opinions and temperaments.

CONFIDENTIALITY

What is said in the group stays in the group.

FAITHFULNESS

We will diligently engage with the material, processing our responses honestly.

OTHER POINTS OF IMPORTANCE TO YOU

_____

_____

_____

THE PARABLE OF THE BUTTERFLY

READ TOGETHER:

> *For the brand-new butterfly, it was like there were two realities in her mind that had no connection to each other.*

> *One was past, a shadow. She remembered days crawling on a single small branch simply eating. There was nothing to do except satisfy the desire to consume. Neither her view or interest went beyond that branch, or even the next leaf. But, why would she want to see further than that anyway? (Cont. overleaf)*

But now she was altogether new. She had these brand-new wings – and she was so uplifted physically and spiritually that she didn't dwell on why it came so naturally to fly as she could. Life now looked completely different, even though her old branch remained below.

Now she could see life beyond the branch to the broad and unconstrained expanse of the garden. This was her new reality and there were no limits here. The garden had always existed of course, she just couldn't see it. Her vision had been constrained and blurred, and her desires focused on that insatiable desire for more.

But now she had to refocus.

A change of perspective had been thrust upon her and life would never look the way it did before. It would be unthinkable to have the gift of flight and yet choose to crawl. She needed to learn how to be compelled by a higher calling now, instead of carnal desire.

Soon she would learn what that calling was.

She was destined to find joy in the garden and be the source of joy for others. She was to know freedom and enjoy fruitfulness. Her story was to be part of something larger than her. She would learn to enhance the garden and enjoy knowing the Gardener.

It was time for her to answer the call to fulfill her design.

Q. Do you see any parallels between the butterfly's shift in vision, and that of believers who determine to look past their own needs and capacities to that of God's grander design?

_____
_____
_____
_____

Q. What do you hope to gain from engaging in this course? What are you looking for regarding the discovery of your calling?

_____
_____
_____
_____

READ TOGETHER:

You might have thought that the caterpillar represents the unredeemed version of a person, and that the butterfly is the new believer. Not so!

1 Corinthians 2:14 – 3:1 defines three states of spiritual maturity that we must traverse:

- **Natural person** (Gk: Psuchikos) – a person who is without the Spirit. An unredeemed person.

- **Carnal person** (Gk: Sarkikos) – a person who is redeemed, yet immature. Led by the old-nature.

- **Spiritual person** (Gk: Pneumatikos) – a person who is predominantly led by the Spirit. A mature believer.

The caterpillar represents the carnal believer. One who has their sights set on their own desires. A true morphing takes place when a believer matures to become led by the Spirit. It is a common next step for them to consider how they can best steward their life to fulfill God's plan. The butterfly represents a spiritual person such as this.

Q. Before you begin reading the course material, try to articulate to the group how you see your calling in Christ. How would you define it? What do you know, and what is missing about what He wants you to be and do?

_____

_____

_____

PRAY FOR EACH OTHER

Take some time discussing the prayer needs of each person in the group and how best you will support them this week.

Finish by praying for one another.

Week 1 – Depth of Calling

Group Session

Use this section at the beginning your 2nd group meeting.

> **INTRODUCTION**
>
> The first group of readings (1.1 through 1.6) sought to reset your perspective on what God has called you to do and be. Rather than self-fulfillment and self-reliance, we are called to pursue and rely on our union with Christ.
>
> Q. What was your overall response to the first week of teaching?
>
> _____
>
> _____
>
> _____
>
> _____
>
> _____
>
> _____
>
> _____
>
> Discuss together your responses from this week's teaching.

[1.1]
Depth of calling

Calling is primarily about living from God, not living for God in your own strength. You are called to something deeper than merely doing.

YOUR RESPONSE:

Q. How have you defined what God's calling would look like for you? Does this chapter change that? How?

_____

_____

_____

_____

_____

_____

_____

[1.2]
A need to re:FOCUS

We need God's help and His perspective to see our calling as we should.

YOUR RESPONSE:

Q. What problem in your life might be better seen as an opportunity or possibility for God to do a work for the kingdom?

_____

_____

_____

_____

_____

_____

_____

_____

_____

[1.3]
Impressive or impacting

Solomon looked back at life from a palace,
Paul from a prison.
Which life and legacy would you choose?

YOUR RESPONSE:

Q. Where has your focus been lately?

Has it been on your own success, or that of others? Is there a focus of your time, energy and passion that needs to be redirected to a more fruitful and eternal cause?

_____

_____

_____

_____

_____

_____

_____

_____

[1.4]

Life in God's garden

*Worldly goals don't correlate to a kingdom calling.
To understand God's plan for you, we must go back to
the beginning.*

YOUR RESPONSE:

Q. At this early stage of the book, how would describe the abundant life Jesus offered? Has any of it been a reality to you? Are there other facets you long for?

_____

_____

_____

_____

_____

_____

_____

_____

[1.5]

Walking and working in the garden

We are called to both faith and deeds, but both must be fueled by our relationship with Christ.

YOUR RESPONSE:

Q. Has your life been both restful and productive? Describe where you are strong in both areas, and if there is a correction that needs to be made.

I am strong in ***walking*** with God in these ways:

_____

_____

_____

_____

_____

_____

_____

_____

I am strong in *working* with God in these ways:

_____

_____

_____

_____

_____

_____

_____

_____

I need to correct that ratio by:

_____

_____

_____

_____

_____

_____

[1.6]

The relational rhythm

Without a close union with Christ, our personal strengths can leave us with less than half of our potential story.

YOUR RESPONSE:

Q. Left to your own devices, are you more inclined to want to do things for God, or enjoy time with God?

_____

_____

Q. Is there anything about your life that would need to adjust in light of today's reading?

_____

_____

CONCLUSION OF GROUP MEETING 2

In closing, pray for each other that Christ would give them clarity in their aspirations and motivations. Seek God for specific grace to guide and provide for where He wants to take each participant.

Week 2 – re:FOCUS on Christ

Group Session

Use this section to introduce your 3rd group meeting.

> **INTRODUCTION**
>
> This week of readings (2.1 through 2.6) focused on rediscovering the most basic element and motivator of Christian endeavor, our intimacy with God.
>
> Q. What was your overall response to this week of readings?
>
> _____
> _____
> _____
> _____
> _____
> _____
>
> Discuss together your responses from this week's teaching.

[2.1]

First

Our commitment to serve God should not outstrip our communion with God.

YOUR RESPONSE:

Q. What phrases would you use to describe your first love for Christ in terms of your relationship, worship and responses to Him when you first came to Christ?

_____

_____

_____

_____

_____

_____

_____

_____

[2.2]

Getting derailed

The two best questions to ask regarding our life's calling are: "Who am I? and "Whose am I?"

YOUR RESPONSE:

Q. How much influence has Christ had in the things that have motivated your ambitions and dreams?

_____

_____

_____

_____

_____

_____

_____

_____

_____

[2.3]
Abiding

Only by dwelling deeply and continually with God do we bear kingdom fruit that lasts.

YOUR RESPONSE:

Q. How well do you believe you are abiding in Christ in this stage of life? In the seasons where you abide most effectively, what is the fruit of that in your life compared to when you are more distant?

_____

_____

_____

_____

_____

_____

_____

_____

[2.4]
Changing lenses

To embrace our next upgrade, we must change our view of what is possible.

YOUR RESPONSE:

Q. Has there been a miracle done in your past, where you have seen God act undeniably to alter a situation? What is it? Do you have faith to see that, and greater things, happen in and through you?

_____

_____

_____

_____

_____

_____

_____

_____

_____

[2.5]
re:FOCUS on Christ

When we look away from Christ, we become practical atheists – believing God can provide, but living like He doesn't.

Your Response:

Q. What possibilities exist for a challenge you currently face? What can you see Jesus doing there? What is He saying about it?

_____

_____

_____

_____

_____

_____

_____

_____

_____

Can you remember what He has done for you before that He can do again?

[2.6]

Living from Christ

As we build our faith through intimacy, we can't help but do extraordinary deeds.

YOUR RESPONSE:

Q. How well are you doing at creating that deep well of faith and love you need to live all that Christ has for you? What has helped and hindered you doing that?

_____

_____

_____

_____

_____

_____

_____

_____

_____

OTHER NOTES:

_____
_____
_____
_____
_____
_____
_____
_____
_____
_____

CONCLUSION OF GROUP MEETING 3

In closing, pray for each other that Christ would give new depth to spiritual intimacy for each participant. Pray that each person would be able to refocus on the presence of God each day, relying on Him for peace and potency to live.

Week 3 – re:FOCUS on Character

Group Session

Use this section to introduce your 4th group meeting.

INTRODUCTION

This week of readings (3.1 through 3.6) focused on becoming the person God has called you to be. What we do will ultimately come from who we are, but are comfortable in our own skin on the journey?

Q. What was your overall response to this week of readings?

_____

_____

_____

_____

_____

Now, discuss together your responses from this week's teaching.

RETREAT AND ADVANCE

For participants who attended a spiritual retreat in the last week.

The days following a time of spiritual refreshment can be somewhat difficult to navigate. Disengaging from normality to spend time with God and His people gives a unique and somewhat unsustainable opportunity to extend our hearts in a deliberate mountain-top experience.

Every mountain casts its own shadow. What happens on Monday when we re-engage with the life we left behind? The same people, problems and stresses are waiting for us. Were my gains valid? What if I didn't experience what I was hoping for? All sorts of questions come to mind.

Good! That is what is supposed to happen. Mountain tops give us a new vision for what normal can look like if we grow over time.

It is not practical to breathe the rarified air of the summit indefinitely — and so we must allow ourselves to fall back and recover. To grow in any area, we must extend past our present sustainable limit, then enter a phase of re-creation. There our spirit grows and adapts, ready to extend again.

This is what a "rhythm of grace" is all about!

Q. What questions and thought processes have arisen in response to your spiritual retreat?

_____
_____
_____
_____
_____
_____
_____
_____
_____
_____
_____
_____
_____
_____
_____
_____
_____
_____
_____

[3.1]
I have made you

Calling is less about what you achieve, and more about who you become.

YOUR RESPONSE:

Q. Is there a goal, or outcome to life that you spend a lot of time thinking about and planning for? Why might your eyes be so fixed on that destination?

_____

_____

_____

_____

_____

_____

_____

_____

_____

[3.2]

Stuck in a moment

Our next step of guidance may well depend on our obedience to the previous one.

YOUR RESPONSE:

Q. What are the things that conspire to keep you stuck in a moment?

_____

_____

_____

_____

_____

_____

_____

_____

_____

[3.3]

Growing character

When all forms of supply are cut off except God Himself – we turn to Him more deeply and grow like Him more fully.

Your Response:

Q. Have you ever been pruned? How did that come about, and what was the long-term result?

_____

_____

_____

_____

_____

_____

_____

_____

[3.4]
The fruit of perseverance

From our worst of circumstance God plans to bring the fruit of hope.

YOUR RESPONSE:

Q. In recent times, have you been able to let suffering do its work in you to produce character and hope?

What was your situation, and how did you respond?

_____

_____

_____

_____

_____

_____

_____

_____

_____

[3.5]
The wilderness effect

Our wilderness is designed to draw us to God – lest we find ourselves in a desert.

YOUR RESPONSE:

Q. Have you ever been through a season in the spiritual wilderness? What were the signs that it was a wilderness?

_____
_____
_____
_____
_____
_____
_____
_____
_____
_____

[3.6]

re:FOCUS on character

Destiny is never focused on the outcome, but the way we take the journey.

YOUR RESPONSE:

Q. What name(s) might encapsulate the identity of who God has been forming you to be throughout your life?

_____

_____

_____

_____

_____

_____

CONCLUSION OF GROUP MEETING 4

In closing, pray for each other that God would reveal more of what He is doing, and who He is forming within each participant.

Week 4 – re:FOCUS on people

Group Session

Use this section to introduce your 5th group meeting.

INTRODUCTION

This week of readings (4.1 through 4.6) encouraged us to let our commitment to those already within our circles of influence become deeper. When we find our people, we have found our purpose.

Q. What was your overall response to this week of readings?

_____

_____

_____

_____

_____

Now, discuss together your responses from this week's teaching.

[4.1]
People are your purpose

When you find your people, you have found your purpose.

YOUR RESPONSE:

Q. Has God ever shown you someone He wants you to invest in? How did He do that, and what was the result?

_____

_____

_____

_____

_____

_____

_____

_____

_____

_____

[4.2]
Your area of influence

God has assigned you a boundary in which you have authority to impact.

YOUR RESPONSE:

Q. Is there a group of people God has placed you in, that you could increasingly bring influence for God? How might you best do that?

_____
_____
_____
_____
_____
_____
_____
_____
_____

[4.3]
You and the church

To find the fullness of God's calling on your life, you also need to find yourself in church.

YOUR RESPONSE:

Q. Where are you serving in the local church?

_____

_____

_____

_____

_____

Q. Is there another way you would like to contribute? What steps could you take to fulfill that?

_____

_____

_____

_____

[4.4]
Oikos

Your greatest calling is to those who are closest to you.

YOUR RESPONSE:

Q. Who are the people in your *oikos*? It is probably between 8-15 who share space with you regularly, and who know the real you. List them out here.

_____

_____

_____

_____

_____

_____

_____

_____

_____

_____

[4.5]
Your tribe

We find unreasonable allegiance from those who wear the same colours.

YOUR RESPONSE:

Q. Who is your tribe? What has it added to your life, and how have you added to those within it?

_____
_____
_____
_____
_____
_____
_____
_____
_____
_____

[4.6]

Re:FOCUS on people

God needs to be the centre of our life and present in all our relationships.

YOUR RESPONSE:

Q. Are any of your circles of influence out of focus? How might you address that?

_____

_____

_____

_____

_____

CONCLUSION OF GROUP MEETING 5

In closing, pray for each other that God would reveal new ways in which each participant can contribute to the lives of those God has given.

Week 5 – re:FOCUS on talent

Group Session

Use this section to introduce your 6th group meeting.

INTRODUCTION

This week of readings (5.1 through 5.6) brought focus on how to give our heart, soul and strength to God.

Q. What was your overall response to this week of readings?

_____

_____

_____

_____

_____

_____

_____

Now, discuss together your responses from this week's teaching.

[5.1]
re:FOCUS on talent

We all have a portfolio of God-given resources to invest in the kingdom.

YOUR RESPONSE:

Q. What skills and experience do you have that God could use for His purpose?

_____

_____

_____

_____

_____

_____

_____

_____

_____

[5.2]

Put your soul in to it

Being faithful in your calling is about investing who you are into the very few things in life that matters.

YOUR RESPONSE:

Q. Are you living out what matters to you and God? Considering where you are required to invest time into career; family; and church, are you satisfied that you have the balance and priorities right for this season of life?

_____

_____

_____

_____

_____

_____

_____

_____

_____

[5.3]
The heart speaks

Your core values determine what you will and won't stand for.

YOUR RESPONSE:

Q. What are the issues and values you will not bend on? Beside each one, try and explain why it matters to you so much.

_____

_____

_____

_____

_____

_____

_____

_____

_____

[5.4]
The need at hand

When looking for your calling, look first to what the world actually needs.

YOUR RESPONSE:

Q. What needs do you see around you that you can contribute to?

a) In your neighborhood:

_____

_____

_____

_____

_____

_____

_____

_____

b) At your work or school:

_____

_____

_____

_____

_____

_____

c) With your family and friends:

_____

_____

_____

_____

_____

_____

[5.5]
Spiritual gifts

Your spiritual gifts bring God-sized fruit from your work with Him.

YOUR RESPONSE:

Q. Do you know what your spiritual gifts are? What are they, and how has God used you in that way?

_____

_____

_____

_____

_____

_____

_____

_____

_____

[5.6]

When doing it for God is not enough

*Trying to fulfill God's will without sticking to God's plan
can leave us high and dry.*

Your Response:

Q. How do you know when you are working from God's strength, and when you are not? Give examples.

_____

_____

_____

_____

_____

_____

_____

_____

CONCLUSION OF GROUP MEETING 6

In closing, pray for each other that God would give increase to the God-given talents and the influence of His Spirit within each participant.

Week 6 – re:FOCUS on calling

Group Session

Use this section to introduce your 7th group meeting.

INTRODUCTION

This week of readings (6.1 through 6.6) was all about making a Plan to re:FOCUS.

Q. What was your overall response to the process?

_____
_____
_____
_____
_____
_____
_____
_____

Before looking at the detail of your Plan to re:FOCUS, look again at the purpose statements that were detailed this week:

re:FOCUS on God – knowing Whose I am

1. I am called to live as a child of God – abiding closely with Christ, drawing my identity and significance from Him.
2. I am called to live as a co-heir with Christ – bearing fruit through the power of His grace working through me.

re:FOCUS on Character – cultivating who I am becoming

3. I am called to be Christ-like – the fruit of the Spirit growing tangibly in my life.
4. I am called by name – being shaped by God into a unique person who is being not just doing.

re:FOCUS on People – influencing those around me

5. I am called to love people – reflecting the heart of God to those around me.
6. I am called to lead people – impacting those in my circle of influence.

re:FOCUS on Talent – giving it everything I have got

7. I am called to use my talents faithfully – loving God with all my heart, soul and strength.
8. I am called to work in the power of God – knowing and using my spiritual gifts.

Q. In which two of these aspects of calling have you been strongest historically?

_____

_____

Q. In which two do you struggle most to find focus?

_____

_____

Discuss together your complete Plan to re:FOCUS.

_____

_____

_____

_____

_____

_____

_____

_____

_____

_____

After discussing together your Plan to re:FOCUS, concluding the meeting and course with prayer for each other.

A Plan to re:FOCUS

RE:FOCUS ON GOD – KNOWING ON WHOSE I AM

Purpose 1:

I am called to live as a child of God - abiding closely with Christ, drawing my identity and significance from Him.

VISION:

In my preferred future, this is how I would like my life to look in regard to this purpose:

_____

_____

_____

_____

GOALS:

To ensure I realise my vision fully in this area, I will:

Strategy: **Achieved by:**

_____ _____

_____ _____

_____ _____

A Plan to re:FOCUS

RE:FOCUS ON GOD – KNOWING ON WHOSE I AM

Purpose 2:

I am called to live as a co-heir with Christ – bearing fruit through the power of His grace working through me.

VISION:

In my preferred future, this is how I would like my life to look in regard to this purpose:

_____

_____

_____

_____

GOALS:

To ensure I realise my vision fully in this area, I will:

Strategy:	Achieved by:
_____	_____
_____	_____
_____	_____

A Plan to re:FOCUS

RE:FOCUS ON CHARACTER – CULTIVATING WHO I AM BECOMING

Purpose 3:

I am called to be Christ-like –
the fruit of the Spirit growing tangibly in my life.

VISION:

In my preferred future, this is how I would like my life to look in regard to this purpose:

_____

_____

_____

_____

GOALS:

To ensure I realise my vision fully in this area, I will:

Strategy:	**Achieved by:**
_____	_____
_____	_____
_____	_____

A Plan to re:FOCUS

RE:FOCUS ON CHARACTER – CULTIVATING WHO I AM BECOMING

Purpose 4:

I am called by name – being shaped by God into a unique person who is being not just doing.

VISION:

In my preferred future, this is how I would like my life to look in regard to this purpose:

_____

_____

_____

_____

_____

GOALS:

To ensure I realise my vision fully in this area, I will:

Strategy: **Achieved by:**

_____   _____

_____   _____

_____   _____

A Plan to re:FOCUS

RE:FOCUS ON PEOPLE – INFLUENCING THOSE AROUND ME

Purpose 5:

I am called to love people –
reflecting the heart of God to those around me.

VISION:

In my preferred future, this is how I would like my life to look in regard to this purpose:

_____

_____

_____

_____

_____

GOALS:

To ensure I realise my vision fully in this area, I will:

Strategy:	Achieved by:
_____	_____
_____	_____
_____	_____

A Plan to re:FOCUS

RE:FOCUS ON PEOPLE – INFLUENCING THOSE AROUND ME

Purpose 6:

*I am called to lead people –
impacting those in my circle of influence.*

VISION:

In my preferred future, this is how I would like my life to look in regard to this purpose:

_____

_____

_____

_____

GOALS:

To ensure I realise my vision fully in this area, I will:

Strategy:	**Achieved by:**
_____	_____
_____	_____
_____	_____

A Plan to re:FOCUS

RE:FOCUS ON TALENT – GIVING IT EVERYTHING I HAVE GOT

Purpose 7:

*I am called to use my talents faithfully –
loving God with all my heart, soul and strength.*

VISION:

In my preferred future, this is how I would like my life to look in regard to this purpose:

_____

_____

_____

_____

GOALS:

To ensure I realise my vision fully in this area, I will:

Strategy: **Achieved by:**

_____   _____

_____   _____

_____   _____

A Plan to re:FOCUS

RE:FOCUS ON TALENT – GIVING IT EVERYTHING I HAVE GOT

Purpose 8:

*I am called to work in the power of God –
knowing and using my spiritual gifts*

VISION:

In my preferred future, this is how I would like my life to look in regard to this purpose:

_____

_____

_____

_____

_____

GOALS:

To ensure I realise my vision fully in this area, I will:

Strategy:	**Achieved by:**
_____	_____
_____	_____
_____	_____

A Plan to re:FOCUS

OTHER IMPORTANT AREAS IN WHICH TO RE:FOCUS

Areas that are vital for me to emphasise.

AREA 1 TO RE:FOCUS: _____

VISION:

In my preferred future, this is how I would like my life to look in regard to this purpose:

_____

_____

_____

_____

_____

GOALS:

To ensure I realise my vision fully in this area, I will:

Strategy:	**Achieved by:**
_____	_____
_____	_____
_____	_____

A Plan to re:FOCUS

OTHER IMPORTANT AREAS IN WHICH TO RE:FOCUS

Areas that are vital for me to emphasise.

AREA 1 TO RE:FOCUS: _____

VISION:

In my preferred future, this is how I would like my life to look in regard to this purpose:

_____

_____

_____

_____

_____

GOALS:

To ensure I realise my vision fully in this area, I will:

Strategy: **Achieved by:**

_____   _____

_____   _____

_____   _____

Notes from your Retreat

Notes from your Retreat

Notes from your Retreat

Notes from your Retreat

Notes from your Retreat

www.ingramcontent.com/pod-product-compliance
Lightning Source LLC
Chambersburg PA
CBHW081421300426
44110CB00017BA/2341